Merry Christmas 2031
from Sue + Bill

CHAUTAUQUA LAKE

MILLER BELL TOWER
PIER BUILDING
COLLEGE CLUB BEACH
CHILDREN'S BEACH
PALESTINE PARK
MT. HERMAN
SHUFFLE BOARD
SPORTS CLUB
BOWLING ON THE GREEN
WENSLEY GUEST HOUSE
ATHENAEUM HOTEL
WOMAN'S CLUB
SOUTH LAKE DRIVE
MILLER
SOUTH TERRACE
HULTQUIST CENTER FOR CONTINUING STUDIES
AMPHITHEATER
BOWMAN
JANES
PECK
COOKMAN
MERRILL
TORY
C.L.S.C. VERANDA
SMITH MEMORIAL LIBRARY
BOY WITH RECORDER
SMITH-WILKES HALL
GOLDEN GATE
PRATT
UNITED CHURCH OF CHRIST
BOWMAN
WAUGH
CARY COTTAGE HOTEL
HALL OF MISSIONS
HALL OF PHILOSOPHY
JANES
PIONEER HALL
C.L.S.C. ALUMNI HALL
PECK
COOKMAN
SOUTH
HALL OF CHRIST
CHAPEL OF THE GOOD SHEPHERD
THUNDER BRIDGE
SOUTH AVE.
YOUTH ACTIVITY CENTER
HEINZ BEACH
SEAVER GYM
BOY'S CLUB
BEESON YOUTH CENTER
GIRL'S CLUB
SHARPE FIELD
PLAY GROUND
TENNIS
SOUTH LAKE DRIVE
COYLE PAVILION
HAWTHORNE
WHITTIER
BRYANT
BOWMAN
WAUGH
MASSEY AVE.
FIRE HALL
MER'S KET
SOUTH GATE PARKING LOT
MASSEY AVE.
MARKET GATE
RTE. 394
SOUTH AVE. GATE
RTE. 394
CHAUTAUQUA GOLF COURSE
GOLF CLUBHOUSE AND PRO SHOP
STOWN AND LAKEWOOD
JANE E. NELSON

TORONTO
ONTARIO
LAKE ONTARIO
HAMILTON
ROCHESTER
BUFFALO
SYRACUSE
NEW YORK
LAKE ERIE
CHAUTAUQUA
JAMESTOWN
ERIE
PENNSYLVANIA
CLEVELAND
OHIO
PITTSBURGH

LAKE ERIE
TO BUFFALO
TO CLEVELAND
I-90
394
424
NEW YORK
CHAUTAUQUA
430
60
394
474
62
WATTSBURG
CORRY
SUGAR GROVE
PENNSYLVANIA
WARREN

A YEAR IN
Chautauqua

Laurie A. Watters

INTRODUCTION BY
Roger Rosenblatt

PARK BENCH PRESS

Photographs on pages 6, 14, 16–19, and 21 are courtesy of
The Chautauqua Institution Archives, Chautauqua, N.Y.

Pages 20 and 22 : *Pen and Picture: A Chautauqua Sketch-Book,*
Edwards, James T. Meadville, PA.: The Chautauqua-Century Press, 1896.

First published in the United States of America in 2000 by
Park Bench Press
Post Office Box 237041
Ansonia Station
New York, New York 10023
WWW.PARKBENCHPRESS.COM

Library of Congress Catalog Card Number: 00-090337
Hardcover ISBN: 0-9677805-0-0

First Edition
10 9 8 7 6 5 4 3 2 1

D.L. TO - 199–2000
PRINTED AND BOUND IN SPAIN

I dedicate this book to two special people in my life

Tootie Watters

Grammy

My Grandmother . . . who has taught me that life is an adventure to be lived

and

Jonathan Nassif

Jon

My husband . . . with whom I look forward to sharing this adventure

Contents

Foreword

THE CHAUTAUQUA INSTITUTION ... impossible to put in words. In my youth I spent summers in Chautauqua. For the past twelve years I have spent as much time there as possible, which is never enough. Over the years, I have been asked often to describe Chautauqua. But I am never able to and always find myself beginning the answer with a sigh and a quick disclaimer—"Chautauqua is very hard to explain." There is something ineffable about it, that something I had not fully understood until I began working on this book—describing Chautauqua does not necessarily explain it.

As a photographer, the idea of capturing Chautauqua on film was simple, but the reality of doing so proved far more challenging. To all who enter its gates, the Chautauqua experience is as unique as the individuals themselves. While the diversity of the experience contributes to its mystery, capturing that diversity on film was the challenge. *A Year in Chautauqua* is my attempt to reveal that which eludes words, and in doing so, pay tribute to this unique place, a place that has profoundly touched so many for so long, myself among them.

The Chautauqua Institution is a cultural, religious, educational, and recreational oasis situated on Chautauqua Lake in the southwest corner of New York State. A summer training ground for young dancers, musicians, actors, and artists; it is also a center of learning that attracts students of all ages, from curious teens to lifelong learners. And mostly it is families, not just mothers and fathers and kids, but grandparents and aunts and uncles and cousins and friends. It is also tennis and golf and sailing, theater, opera, classrooms, and dance. Chautauqua too is pastel cottages, rocking chairs on wraparound porches, American flags, and red brick walks in the shade of thousands of trees. It is porch-sitting with a good book or a summer friend. It is an early morning bike ride for local corn and flowers at the farmers market; the Amphitheater alive with ideas and music and applause. It is an afternoon nap. Mornings at Chautauqua belong to the lecture series, and evenings to the performing arts. Performances vary from the Chautauqua Symphony to the Beach Boys; from the ballet to the Tommy Dorsey Orchestra; and from Marcel Marceau to Mark Russell. It is rules and gate passes and order too. It is guest houses, hotels, shops, and churches; the library, the post office, the bookstore, all cheek to jowl with some of Chautauqua's original buildings, which date back to the late 19th century. Quintessentially American, Chautauqua gives one the feeling of walking into a Norman Rockwell painting. In 1905, Theodore Roosevelt described Chautauqua as "the most American place in America."

So it was my goal to capture the spirit of Chautauqua on the pages that follow. It's clear to me now that Chautauqua is a place that must be experienced to be truly understood and, once experienced, a place that never leaves you. It is my hope that this book will provide Chautauquans with a keepsake, entice those who have never been, and share with those who may never wander through its gates.

Introduction

O NE AUGUST EVENING, on my third or fourth visit to Chautauqua, I wandered down to the amphitheater to hear a concert, which was already in progress. Instead of taking a seat right away, I stood at an entrance near the stage and took a long look at the audience. This was different from looking at an audience while speaking from the stage. I felt no tension or self-consciousness; only pleasure in studying the rows of faces, which, as I watched, became a collective painting—something out of the Old Masters—alive and gleaming in lantern-light against the muted colors of their clothing, and the night.

For the first time, I really saw Chautauqua. Until that moment I had been thinking of the institution merely as enlightened series of events—an intellectual-cum-artistic circus hauled together in sleepy upstate New York to help amiable and informed people pass the summer. Or, if not that, then as a sort of hectic Shangri-La in which the residents stayed young by making the lecturers grow old. Speaker beware: when invited to Chautauqua, do not assume you will get away with a single performance. Prepare yourself for the radio station, the local papers, the relentlessly inquisitive Chautauqua Literary and Scientific Circle, and any number of charming but zealous individuals fully capable of grabbing you by the lapels, as you stroll a path, and reordering your life.

But on the evening of that concert, I began to peer into the heart of Chautauqua, which is a capacious and complex heart made up of subtle instruments of giving and receiving. The amphitheater, as anyone knows who has been lucky enough to sit there, is a large, open musical instrument. Sound reverberates there like the insides of a cello. The audience I watched that night was so deeply appreciative of the music, they seemed to become partners in creating it. So it is with most everything at Chautauqua. The place is made up of people who fuse with the music, the lectures, the art, the cottages, the lake, the porches, paths, flowers, hedges, shadows, and with one another in a single, identifiable heart.

All this Laurie Watters has discovered and made beautiful in her book of photographs. Like most visitors, I have seen only one season at Chautauqua, *the* season. She has captured an entire Year at Chautauqua, which extends one's view to more than nine additional months. The book gives a sense of the continuity of the community, and of other natural continuities. Wooden steps in autumn are not the same as wooden steps in summer; they look stiffer, more solitary, less like kids. On the other hand, hedges frosted with snow look more playful and attractive than good old summer hedges. The light changes, outfits change; an open window shuts. The tree that is shagged with ice will bloom like broccoli; count on it. The road will freeze and thaw again.

Like all first-rate artist-photographers, Watters makes us want to see what we have always seen. She is not interested in tricks or shocks. She has better ideas—like focusing on the concentration of various people reading newspapers; on wedding celebrations; on bikes and dogs. Here is the significance of the commonplace:

a trellis is no less inspiring that a clock tower or the monumental Athenaeum Hotel. Watters gives us not simply a porch—there are many different porches in the book—but the *idea* of a porch. One recognizes the structure as an outdoor room located between a closed house and the wider world, allowing equally for observation and contemplation. This structure is a perfect emblem of the Chautauquan mind.

There is a danger when attempting to describe or depict a place like Chautauqua (is there another?). One runs the risk of giving the impression of preciousness, isolation and exclusivity. And, to be sure, this is no ordinary community; it was drawn together not only by historical and familial traditions, but also by certain commonalties of taste and a desired style and pace of living. The special quality of Chautauqua, though, derives from a breadth, not a narrowness, of vision—an appreciation for all of life and life's seasons. This, too, is conveyed by Watters. Chautauqua is still a spiritual place. It may be Methodist in origin, but it is catholic in perspective, as open to the casual normalities as to intense and lofty moments.

Watters makes lofty moments of the normalities—the guys in a marathon; the kids in the water or on their sleds; an older woman carrying groceries at her side, raising an umbrella as she walks on a path shining with rain. It is all very quiet and familiar, and at the same time raucous and strange. What world of thought does the girl licking the ice-cream cone occupy? What goes through the head of the white-bearded fellow in the patriotic top hat and the false nose? Everything stands alone and is part of the whole. In an open window with paint peeling on the ledge stands a row of compatible apples and oranges.

Given my experience on the night of the concert, I am especially taken with the picture of a Chautauqua audience in the amphitheater, photographed from the back, not as I studied my audience that summer night. Here is a full house, as usual, a gathered population both active and receptive, remarkable and plain as daylight. I wish that I could see their faces. But, of course, I can.

TENT PLATFORM

In Chautauqua's early years,
tents provided shelter for
attendees.

Chautauqua is an idea embracing the "all things" of life—art, science, society, religion, patriotism, education—whatsoever intends to enlarge, refine and ennoble the individual, to develop domestic charm and influence, to make the nation stronger and wiser, and to make Time and Eternity seem to be what they are—parts of one noble and everlasting whole.

—JOHN HEYL VINCENT

The Chautauqua Story

JONATHAN NASSIF

FOR MORE THAN 125 YEARS the Chautauqua Institution has held to the course charted by its founders, John Heyl Vincent, an Illinois Methodist minister, and Lewis Miller, an Ohio industrialist. Remarkably unchanged, both in spirit and practice, since its beginnings in 1874, Chautauqua remains a reflection of American popular culture at its most sublime. Long recognized for its influence on education, religion, public policy, and the arts, the Chautauqua program continues to be anchored to 19th-century Christian values and social idealism.

Located in southwestern New York State, 60 miles south of Buffalo and 50 miles east of Erie, Pennsylvania, the Chautauqua Institution is a not-for-profit organization run by a 24-member board of trustees. It currently operates for a period of nine weeks called "the season" from the end of June through the last week of August. This gated community has 7,500 summertime and 400 year-round residents but sees more than 150,000 visitors pass through its gates over the course of a season. Gate passes are mandatory for both residents and visitors during the season and entitle the holder to concerts, lectures, various performances, recitals, religious services, and art exhibits. People also come to enjoy the lake, its beaches, and other recreational facilities in a most unique environment.

At its inception those who came to Chautauqua were Protestant, generally middle class, middle aged, and urban. Traditional schooling, such as it was in the mid-19th century, had come to an end for many early on. No longer tied to the plow, with a bit of time and money to spare, they were drawn to Chautauqua to read, study, and receive instruction in their faith with like-minded people in a bucolic summer setting. They came for a day, a week, or a season and returned home intellectually and spiritually invigorated. Deeply rooted in the conviction that education for everyone benefits not only the individual spirit but that of the community and the nation—particularly a nation so recently and tragically demoralized by the horrors of civil war—Chautauqua's beginnings were simple, its ambitions modest, but the idea itself was revolutionary.

Lewis Miller was born on July 24, 1829, in Greentown, Ohio. From an early age he had an eagerness for education, its methods and philosophy. He received the usual country schooling in reading, writing, and arithmetic; and by the age of 16 was himself a teacher in a rural school. But it was Miller's distaste for the family business of farming—an occupation that demanded too much work and left him too little time for study—that spurred him to change the course of his life. At 20, without experience as a craftsman or inventor, Miller left home for Plainfield,

Illinois, where, with a few relatives, he opened a farm implement shop. Talent is often liberated by circumstance, and before long Miller was successfully marketing his own equipment. By the time he was 26, he held a patent for the Buckeye Mower, highly praised both for its innovation and utility. More inventions quickly followed, and with them fame and fortune. In time though, apparently unchallenged by his success, Miller grew restless. "He wanted something more universal. He wanted books. He wanted to know."

Through his years of success Miller remained, as he put it, "as good a Methodist as I can be." In 1863, he joined the First Methodist Church of Akron, Ohio, taking

LEWIS MILLER (1829–1899)

JOHN HEYL VINCENT (1832–1920)

an active role in the Sunday school program. Miller's flair for management, coupled with his love for education, naturally led him to take on the restructuring of the Sunday school program. When asked to be the superintendent of the program he eagerly accepted, quickly making it the most exceptional educational system in the city. He introduced graded classes and called for weekly teachers' conferences, he reworked the Bible-intensive curriculum to include science and nature. Laymen were recruited to teach alongside clergy, to lend practical support to the church theories, thus generating a broader appeal. These were the seeds of a curriculum that would later blossom at the Chautauqua Assembly.

John Heyl Vincent was born in Tuscaloosa, Alabama, February 23, 1832. Like Miller, he was precocious, driven, and restless from an early age. His ministry, reported by Rebecca Richmond in her book *Chautauqua,* is said to have begun when he was just six years old. With a bible in one hand and fishing rod in the other, he would share the gospel with black children from his neighborhood by reading stories to the small congregation.

Religion was a defining influence in shaping young Vincent's mind. His mother and father were devoted Methodists and active in the local church. More than simply setting aside daily time for prayer, his parents would frequently initiate religious discussions among the family, and occasionally guests from the local Baptist, Calvinist, and Second Adventist ministries would visit. In the energized atmosphere, lively discussions on any given religious themes took place. Vincent, still a child, would quietly listen, gaining most, one could say, in receiving a religious education that was remarkably tolerant and open to a variety of perspectives.

Vincent suffered though, like many a thoughtful young person would, when faced with the complexities and prescriptions of a religious fundamentalist upbringing. Education, too, was a source of pain for him—it was at once his "idol" and his nemesis. Struggling to find a proper balance between the church and the classroom, he tried to reconcile the worldly motives of education with the selflessness of Christian living. Early on, it was his appetite for knowledge and the life of the mind that triumphed—reading extensively in history, philosophy, and literature. But later his perspective changed and he determined that pastoral work was the superior calling. It was the death of Vincent's mother in 1852 that was the turning point, leading him to abandon the idea of college and begin his ministry—a calling characterized by its focus on making religious education accessible to anyone who desired it and improving the quality of work done by Sunday school teachers. In his ministry he traveled extensively, and in 1865 established the *Sunday-School Quarterly*, a monthly journal that forged new methods for instructing teachers.

Perhaps it was inevitable these two visionaries would join forces. Kindred spirits, both shared a soul-burning love for learning. Neither attended college, both were products of the same age and religious upbringing; both were education activists, leaders in the field of Sunday school reform; and both saw the social and spiritual value of secular and religious synthesis.

In the early part of 1873 Vincent and Miller met, unceremoniously, at an afternoon session of a Sunday school conference. Their enthusiasm for each other's ideas and mutual admiration for each other's intellect were immediately recognized. At this very first meeting with their plans for a new program—one that would take the shape of a two-week session of meetings and conferences on related themes, with lectures and sermons by national leaders, and most importantly, advanced training for Sunday school teachers— the *Chautauqua* idea emerged.

The idea, however, was in want of a setting. Miller suggested holding the first sessions at Fair Point on Chautauqua Lake. A trustee of the

PIER BUILDING

The original Pier Building was constructed in 1886 on an area initially called Fair Point.

Camp Meeting Association, which held rights to the land, Miller believed that the isolation of Fair Point, with its natural beauty, was better suited to worship and study than were the artifice and clamor of the city. Vincent disagreed. He felt the site was not only too difficult to reach, but also had grave doubts about holding the assembly on the site of a camp meeting. Camp meetings, which had been held in the United States since 1799, were rooted in religious fundamentalism, more tied to emotion than reasoned thought. For Vincent, the camp meeting did not represent the sober, thoughtful element of church life that he envisioned for his assembly. Miller argued that their assembly would be different and talked Vincent into seeing Fair Point for himself. The rest is history.

ASSEMBLY GROUNDS

The speakers platform was used by the Chautauqua Assembly beginning in 1874. The poles standing at the end of the benches supported boxes of earth in which torches were secured during the evening assemblies.

MILLER COTTAGE
CIRCA 1875

This Swiss chalet–style cottage, built by Lewis Miller, is located on the edge of the former assembly grounds, now called Miller Park. The striped tent to the right of the front porch served as a men's dormitory.

Fair Point sat on the shore of Chautauqua Lake. The camp was situated in a clearing in the woods, with footpaths leading to the most basic of buildings designated for study. Tents for living were placed on platforms on the perimeter of what is now known as Miller Park. In and around the trees, benches were laid out in rows to accommodate the thousands of people who attended the first two-week session. In the evenings, bonfires, torches, and lanterns illuminated the sylvan background, the flickering golden light playing on and off the faces of those held in rapt attention.

On August 4, 1874, Vincent led a "Covenant Service" outlining their noble and serious mission. Presbyterian, Baptist, and Methodist preachers alike followed with an enthusiastic endorsement of the plan, confirming the defining mission of the all-denominational enterprise. The sessions that first season centered exclusively on Sunday school. Never before had so many representatives of Sunday schools gathered for such a long period of time. Teachers and administrators alike were instructed on matters of curriculum, particularly the integration of Bible studies with secular disciplines, teacher training, and parish politics. Given the opportunity to speak freely, criticisms, positive and negative, were welcomed, even problems relating to the church could be openly discussed.

From the beginning, Miller and Vincent were intent on distancing their Fair Point Assembly (as it was called in these early days) from the revivalistic Sunday camp meetings which continued to meet at Fair Point when the Assembly was not in session. It was clear to them that camp meetings were motivated more by commercialization and entertainment than by worship and study. Responding quickly to the threat of the meetings' compromising influence, the Fair Point Assembly decided to close the gates to all visitors on Sunday, curtailing access to the grounds from both the road and the lake.

Other Assembly departures from the camp meeting traditions included a prohibition against unauthorized meetings, more structured and comprehensive exercises, and the implementation of a gate fee, mostly to cover the expenses incurred by scheduling popular evangelists and prominent lay speakers.

The Assembly format was enthusiastically embraced and by the third year, operating as the Chautauqua Assembly, the program was extended to 24 days and divided into four sessions: the existing Sunday school conference and three additional conferences. The 1876 Assembly season included a scientific conference, which featured Miller's son-in-law, Thomas Alva Edison, lecturing on his latest experiments in artificial illumination; a temperance conference, honoring the Women's Christian Temperance Union—formed two

years earlier in Chautauqua—whose work led to the signing of the 18th Amendment to the Constitution (to this day, Chautauqua forbids the sale of alcoholic beverages); and a church congress, which included a visit from Ulysses S. Grant (the first of nine United States presidents to visit Chautauqua). It is astonishing that in only its third year the Chautauqua Assembly would host world figures of enduring importance.

Chautauqua continues to uphold this reputation for attracting leaders in their field. One of the most important and enduring traditions of each season is the morning lecture held each weekday in Chautauqua's historic amphitheater. "The Amp," as it is affectionately called, has served as a bully pulpit for the ideas of many of the century's most influential minds, among them, Alexander Graham Bell, Jonas Salk, Amelia Earhart, Booker T. Washington, Helen Keller, William Jennings Bryan, Susan B. Anthony, and Charles Lindbergh. Some highlights have been John D. Rockefeller, Jr.'s lecture on capital and labor in 1918, and Franklin D. Roosevelt's "I Hate War" speech on his third visit, August 14, 1936.

While tremendously enthusiastic about their project and where it was headed, by the end of the third year Miller and Vincent recognized that a division of labor was necessary to meet the changing needs of an ever-increasing and diverse crowd. Miller, with a background more suited to business, took the title of president (a position he held until his death in 1899), while Vincent took over the responsibilities for the educational program. But dividing labor did not mean dividing authority, as both men felt such a move would only "have slowed down the machinery." So strong was their commitment to work together that they signed a statement saying in effect that no successes at Chautauqua could be credited to one without the other. An added level of organization and focus resulted, and by the fourth year the Assembly program endeavored to include more secular topics, directing attention to issues of political, social, literary, and economic concern. Lectures increased twofold from the previous year, and now both educational and inspirational programs were in place with a clear line distinguishing the two.

Constantly seeking to strengthen and extend the educational program, Vincent struck upon an idea, the ramifications of which would change the scope of Chautauqua's influence: the Chautauqua Literary and Scientific Circle (CLSC) was organized in 1878. Through correspondence instruction from professors, monthly reports, and assigned reading, the CLSC offered the opportunity for lifelong learning by granting access to educational resources traditionally available only to those affiliated with a college or university. *The Chautauqua Assembly Daily Herald* (today, *The Chautauquan Daily*) of August 8, 1882, announced it as "the first systematic

CLSC GOLDEN GATE
CIRCA 1882

On recognition day, graduates of the Chautauqua Literary and Scientific Circle march through a "Golden Gate," installed annually for the ceremony.

plan for correspondence instruction in this country." Articles in *The Chautauquan,* a monthly magazine, formed a part of the assigned reading. A few years later, the Chautauqua Press, the forerunner of university presses, published the CLSC course books. The CLSC has been called the oldest continuing book club in America and serves as the model for correspondence schools today.

The idea for the CLSC extended beyond the limitations of the summer season and harkened back to the days when Vincent himself had wanted to study without the restrictions of a campus and its expense. In many communities throughout the land CLSC membership provided the only means possible for broadening one's cultural outlook. As a result of the popularity and the growing influence of Chautauqua's secular and religious programming, hundreds of similar independent communities sprang up around the country. Each motivated by a longing to learn, they became a part of what is now called the Chautauqua Movement.

HALL OF PHILOSOPHY
CIRCA 1879

The Hall of Philosophy was built for the use of the Chautauqua Literary and Scientific Circle.

In realizing that no center dedicated to human enrichment would be complete without a formidable arts program, Vincent saw fit to enhance the already thriving educational and inspirational curriculum. While music in Chautauqua was present from the beginning, it wasn't until 1879 that significant energy would be given to developing its agenda. The newly built Amphitheater provided some of the impetus, quickly becoming the principal gathering spot for musical entertainment. Twenty-two music classes were slated for this year, and seven concerts were scheduled in a move toward expanding instrumental performance and study. In 1893 William H. Sherwood, "America's foremost piano virtuoso" and student of Franz Liszt, was hired to head the music department. Through his personal teaching and weekly recitals he established Chautauqua as a preeminent center for music. Today music is at the heart of the nine-week season appealing to both popular and classical tastes, and Chautauqua is said to be "the longest running music festival in America."

Nine years after the death of John Vincent in 1920, opera made its debut at Chautauqua. On July 19, 1929, Norton Memorial Hall opened with a performance of Flotow's *Martha* in front of an audience that included Mrs. Thomas Edison and

Henry Ford. The reception was enthusiastic, and the company went on to perform a total of five operas in 1929, adding to the well-known concert, symphony, and choir series.

In 1946 the writers' workshop was introduced under the direction of John Holmes, the noted Johns Hopkins University poet. Courses that ranged in length from one-day workshops to nine-week classes were planned for instruction in both verse and prose. Over the years such distinguished writers as popular essayist Rollo Walter Brown, novelist Margaret Widdemer, and poet Oscar Williams contributed to the program.

Today, a summer of intensive study is offered students on the verge of professional careers through Chautauqua's four schools of fine and performing arts (music, dance, theater, and the visual arts). In addition, over 400 open-enrollment classes offer a wide range of interests for all ages, such as foreign languages, finance, and personal development.

At Chautauqua, education and vacation have

long been synonymous, but an additional and vital part of Miller and Vincent's original vision was time for leisure. By the third year of the Assembly, swimming, boating, even a roller skating rink, and a short time later, a roller coaster at the far end of the grounds, were added to the delight of the children. Today recreation and sports of nearly every type are represented at Chautauqua. The waterfront offers a lively mix of boating, fishing, swimming, and sunning. Other activities to choose from include tennis, golf, basketball, softball, shuffleboard, and lawn bowling. But when it comes to leisure, nothing appeals to one's well-being as much as riding a bicycle or walking the grounds.

Though it has become a more complex and diversified community than even the founders may have envisioned, Chautauqua continues to be guided by their ideas. This is clearly evidenced in the "Chautauqua Challenge" of today, adopted by the board of trustees in 1976:

TO BE A CENTER *for the identification and development of the best in human values through a program which:* ENCOURAGES *the identification and exploration of the value dimensions in the important religious, social and political issues of our times;* STIMULATES *the provocative, thoughtful, involvement of individuals and families in creative response to such issues on a high level of competence and commitment;* PROMOTES *excellence and creativity in the appreciation, performance and teaching of the arts.*

TO BE A COMMUNITY *in which religious faith is perceived, interpreted and experienced as central to the understanding and expression of our social and cultural values, and which, while open to all, is distinctly founded upon and expressive of the convictions of the Christian tradition.*

TO BE A RESOURCE *for the enriched understanding of the opportunities and obligations of community, family and personal life by fostering the sharing of varied cultural, educational, religious and recreational experience in an atmosphere of participation by persons of all ages and backgrounds.*

The legacy of Lewis Miller and John Heyl Vincent is secure because in their genius they found a way to insure that the more Chautauqua changes the more it remains the same.

At the risk of distorting the scope of the Chautauqua story, I have left out many names, places, and dates in favor of focusing on its origins. The spark, I believe, that ignites the idea at the heart of Chautauqua, setting it apart from flawed utopian plans, is the extraordinary social, religious, and educational inclusivity envisioned by its founders.

I am indebted to the following authors for providing me their complete pictures of Chautauqua: Theodore Morrison, *Chautauqua: A Center of Education, Religion, and the Arts in America*; Alfreda Irwin, *Three Taps of the Gavel: Pledge to the Future*; Rebecca Richmond, *Chautauqua: An American Place*; John Vincent, *The Chautauqua Movement*; Jesse L. Hurlbut, *The Story of Chautauqua*.

Springtime in Chautauqua brings

the smells of . . .

new blossoms, musty cottages after winter hibernation, freshly cut grass, and

the sounds of . . .

dripping icicles, hammering of nails, whizzing of fishing lines at dawn, peeping

ducklings, exchange of wedding vows, splashing of fish feeding, tuning of the

Massey Organ, and the chimes of the Miller Bell Tower.

THE MILLER BELL TOWER

The most recognizable
landmark and the symbol
of Chautauqua, the Miller
Bell Tower sits on an area
initially called Fair Point.

SUNSET ON CHAUTAUQUA LAKE

Chautauqua Lake

The name Chautauqua Lake is thought to be derived from an Indian word meaning "bag tied in the middle," which describes its shape. The 18,000-acre lake is divided into the upper lake (north), a deeper basin with depths of up to 75 feet, and the lower basin (south), with a shallower depth of up to 20 feet. It is connected by narrows at Bemus Point.

Chautauqua Lake sits 1,400 feet above sea level, stretches eighteen miles, and has an average width of 1.2 miles. Interestingly, the lake does not drain into Lake Erie, only eight miles and 726 feet below, but rather into the Gulf of Mexico via the Chadakoin, Conewango, Allegheny, Ohio, and Mississippi rivers.

The Chautauqua Institution, located on the northern end of the lake, is bordered on one side by its 1.5-mile shoreline.

SUNRISE ON CHAUTAUQUA LAKE

(OVERLEAF) NORTH LAKE DRIVE

Strolling the Grounds

Chautauquans stroll along the pathways and promenades that wind through the 225 acres referred to as "The Grounds."

48 SOUTH LAKE CIRCA 1894

A lakeside cottage with a second-story wraparound sleeping porch.

4 PROSPECT AVENUE

This house across from University Hill was built in 1991. Although contemporary, it incorporates established architectural features like the gabled roof with decorative bargeboards.

15 NORTH LAKE DRIVE
CIRCA 1883

This double-turreted tower cottage is one of the oldest. It is located in the Miller Park historic area.

Chautauqua Architecture

Most of the 1,100 cottages scattered around the grounds are privately owned, some by eighth-generation families.

Beautiful examples of late 19th- and early 20th-century architecture mixed with contemporary styles are abundant as one explores the grounds. Victorian, Greek and Gothic Revival, Italianate, Stick Style, Mansard, Queen Anne, and Neo-Georgian styles are all represented. A combination of these architectural features decorated with gables, knops, turrets, balustrades, columns, cupolas, porticos, and gingerbread all contribute to Chautauqua's charm.

Porches

Cottages were designed for outdoor living. The ubiquitous Chautauqua front porch is an outdoor sitting room often decorated with wicker furniture, wall hangings, rugs, hanging flower baskets, and gladiolus, which stand in vases during the summer.

17 WHITTIER AVENUE

12 PECK AVENUE

41 NORTH LAKE DRIVE

(OVERLEAF) MOONRISE OVER CHAUTAUQUA LAKE

Purple Martin Bird Houses

Because Purple Martins nest only in man-made housing, the Chautauqua Bird, Tree and Garden Club has installed houses for them along the lake. The Purple Martins, along with Chautauqua's Little Brown Bats (*myotis lucifugus*), keep the insect population under control.

The side terrace of this
house is perched over the
lake. Previously owned by
the Institution, this home
once served as the presiden-
tial residence.

RED BRICK WALK

Looking toward the
Amphitheater where Janes
Avenue crosses the Red
Brick Walk.

ATHENAEUM HOTEL

The baroque staircase leading
up to the lakeside veranda of
the Athenaeum Hotel was
added during 1983 renovations.

PIONEER HALL CIRCA 1885

The first graduating class (1882) of the Chautauqua Literary and Scientific Circle (CLSC) donated this building. This Gothic Revival–style building now shelters a collection of CLSC artifacts and memorabilia.

45

Chautauqua

Chautauqua is many things to many people; it is the unfolding of an idea . . . a summer vacation with a purpose. Ample testimony to the power and appeal of coming together to study, worship, create and play . . . holding together the vision of faith and learning . . . a serious and studious picnic on a gigantic scale.

Quotes from various authors and speakers
Chautauqua Impressions
by Richard N. Campen

Preparations

Springtime in Chautauqua is a time to anticipate the coming summer season. Many last-minute projects are completed, since major construction is not permitted in season. Putting in the docks during the spring and taking them out in the fall are biannual Chautauqua tasks.

THE RENOVATED GIRLS' CLUB
ON SOUTH LAKE DRIVE,
ORIGINALLY BUILT IN 1902

FOUNTAIN ON BESTOR PLAZA

PIER BUILDING CIRCA 1916

In the beginning, most visitors arrived here almost hourly by steamboat. The original Pier Building, built in 1886, housed the clock tower and chimes. Today the College Club is located in the Pier Building and is a gathering place for college-age Chautauquans.

CARNAHAN-JACKSON DANCE STUDIO CIRCA 1912

Originally, this building was an infirmary. Following a series of transformations it was converted in 1986 and today is the home of the Chautauqua School of Dance.

PRACTICE VILLAGE

Each of the 52 practice studio "shacks" is named for a famous composer, including George Gershwin, who composed his Concerto in F in 1925 while visiting Chautauqua. Every studio contains a piano for use by the Chautauqua School of Music students and members of the Chautauqua Symphony Orchestra.

*Chautauqua has been called unique even more often than
she has been called beautiful.*
—Alfreda L. Irwin, Chautauqua historian

Weddings

On any given weekend,
pre- and post-season,
bridal parties parade along
the Red Brick Walk.

COOKMAN AVENUE

"Dixie" cottage, with its pink and white trim, is located at 5 Thompson Avenue.

CENTER AVENUE

Center Avenue looking toward the Main Gate Welcome Center.

FISHING NORTH OF THE MILLER BELL TOWER

Summertime in Chautauqua brings

the smells of . . .

Barbeques, fresh-cut gladiolus on porches, suntan lotion, lake algae in August, and

the sounds of . . .

the practice shacks alive with music, operatic voices, clinking of shrouds hitting
sailboat masts in the breeze, applause, Thunder Bridge, piano scales, bang of the
start gun during weekly sailboat races, mélange of voices lecturing on a variety of
topics, crackling of thunder, hushed conversations around the Amp's perimeter,
hissing of July 4th flares, motorboats, 6:00 PM Fire Department siren, "Holy, Holy,
Holy . . . Lord God Almighty" floating from the Amphitheater, splashing of tod-
dlers at the Children's Beach, whooshing of bats eating bugs at twilight, cracking
of softballs from Sharpe Field, chitchat on the Brick Walk, steam whistle of the
Chautauqua Belle, the morning song "Onward Boys' Club . . . Onward Girls' Club"
piercing the still morning air, the Chautauqua Symphony, and the chimes
of the Miller Bell Tower.

Summer (The Season)

THE MILLER BELL TOWER

AERIAL VIEW OF THE MILLER
BELL TOWER

The Main Gate

The original main gate was constructed in 1917 to serve the increasing number of visitors arriving by auto and on the Mayville-Jamestown rail line.

The Main Gate Welcome Center is now the principal portal for visitors. The Welcome Center, reconfigured and expanded in 1997, contains the main ticket office, hospitality, accommodations, and the Chautauqua County Visitors Bureau.

Gate tickets are required to enter and exit the grounds during the season.

SOUTH GATE

The Chautauquan Daily

During the morning hours the familiar cry of "get your *Chautauquan Daily* here"
can be heard as young Chautauquans peddle the daily newspaper. *The Chautauquan Daily*
dates back to 1876, when it was *The Chautauqua Assembly Daily Herald*. In 1906 *The
Herald* changed its name to *The Chautauquan Daily*. *The Daily* continues to be published
only during the season and keeps Chautauquans informed of what is happening throughout the Institution.

The "village green," named
to honor longtime President,
Arthur Eugene Bestor
(1915–1944).

9 MERRILL AVENUE

17 ROBERTS AVENUE

BESTOR PLAZA

Bestor Plaza, surrounded by the Colonnade Building, Bookstore, Post Office, Refectory, St. Elmo, and library, is the heart of Chautauqua. On this particular summer day the Chautauqua Community Band plays for a crowd at lunch time.

Playing with the water spouting from the mouths of Bestor Fountain fish sculptures continues to fascinate children.

THE CHAUTAUQUA COMMUNITY BAND

11 NORTH LAKE

This board-and-batten architecture dates back to 1895. Its name describes the building system in which weathered boards are mounted vertically. The cracks are then sealed with milled strips called battens.

19 McCLINTOCK AVENUE
CIRCA 1887

This vernacular-style cottage, with decorative window boxes, follows a Chautauqua tradition of flying the American flag.

50 SOUTH LAKE: HEINZ
COTTAGE CIRCA 1900

39 NORTH LAKE

This cottage, with its Dutch
architectural influence, was
built in 1902 by Clement
Studebaker's father, the auto-
mobile manufacturer.

Chautauqua Children's School

Nursery school education was pioneered at Chautauqua. Today the Children's School continues to offer a wide range of activities for three- to five-year-olds.

PARADE

The July 4th Children's School Parade is a 100-year-old Chautauqua tradition.

(OVERLEAF)
AMPHITHEATER AUDIENCE

The Amphitheater

The "Amp," built in 1893, is the oldest open-air, covered amphitheater still in use today. The hub of summer programming, the Amp serves as concert hall, lecture platform, and a nondenominational house of worship. Its wooden bench pews descend to ground level with seating capacity of 5,000.

Three nights weekly the 77-member Chautauqua Symphony Orchestra performs in the Amphitheater. Sounds of the symphony have filled the night air since 1929.

THE CHOIR

The Chautauqua Choir averages 120 members who sing for the Sunday morning worship service. Roughly 35 are members of the Motet Choir, which is an auditioned choir. The remaining members need only attend two of the three rehearsals prior to Sunday.

Some of the pipes of the Massey Memorial Organ can be seen behind the choir. Located in the Amphitheater, this is the largest "outdoor" organ in the world. The organ contains 5,628 pipes ranging in length from 32 feet to half the size of a straw.

THE RALEIGH RINGERS

A guest bell choir plays at the
Sunday worship service.

RAINY DAYS CAN BE MAGICAL IN CHAUTAUQUA

RED BRICK WALK

No bicycles or cars are allowed on the Red Brick Walk, which winds through the Institution and connects many of its major venues.

WINDOW ON THE ARTS & CRAFTS QUADRANGLE

Chautauqua School of Art

The Chautauqua School of Art offers an intensive summer study program for students on the verge of professional careers. These students are selected for admittance to the program.

Throughout the summer, the school also offers open-enrollment classes, including ceramics, sculpture, painting, drawing, and weaving.

The Athenaeum Hotel
CIRCA 1881

This "Grande Dame" of Chautauqua stands on a slight elevation commanding spectacular views beyond its sprawling front lawn to the lakefront.

At the Athenaeum Hotel, meals can be taken either in its grand dining room or on its majestic lakefront veranda. At dinner men are required to wear jacket and tie and women are asked to dress in their finest, a tradition continued from the elegant past. A choice of two desserts after dinner is a favorite of the hotel guests.

Sitting on Rockers

. . . A cool breeze coupled with the gentle motion of the chairs create a serene lull in the afternoon. This escape makes the outside world seem so far away. Here is a place to return year after year. It remains timeless. Yes, there are outer changes. Yes, the grounds are expanding. But, there seems to be a consistency found here that one finds only at home. Or is this home?

Porches of Chautauqua by Anne-Marie D'Agostino

Daniel L. Bratton, serving the third-longest tenure as president of the Chautauqua Institution, cheers on runners.

OLD FIRST NIGHT RUN

Over 600 runners of all ages participate in the annual Old First Night Run/Walk. The course follows the 2.6-mile perimeter loop of the grounds.

Old First Night: Chautauqua's Annual Birthday Celebration

Young Chautauquans present master of ceremonies Richard Karslake with a donation to the Chautauqua Fund on behalf of the Children's School.

OLD FIRST NIGHT TRADITION

George "Shorty" Follansbee, a member of a five-generation Chautauqua family, has been an usher in the Amphitheater since 1932. Receiving the collection baskets on Old First Night is a tradition.

AIR BAND

The Boys' and Girls' Club Air Band performance is a popular event on the Amphitheater stage during the Old First Night program.

16 PECK AVENUE

Built in the 1880s, this is Chautauqua's one and only log cabin.

10 MORRIS AVENUE: THUMBELINA COTTAGE

Delicately designed balustrades decorate this tiny cottage tucked away behind Bestor Plaza.

19 PALESTINE: "TOP-O-THE HILL" CIRCA 1881

These stacked porches have great views of the Amphitheater stage.

LAKESIDE LODGE

Looking through the Oval Garden on the north side of the Athenaeum Hotel to the Lakeside Lodge.

32 SOUTH LAKE

Perhaps the most photographed cottage, this irregularly shaped Victorian home was built in 1883. It is nestled between the Chautauqua Women's Club and the United Methodist Missionary House seen in the background.

GOLDEN GATE

On Recognition Day a "Golden Gate" is installed at the lakeside entrance to the Hall of Philosophy. The parade passes through the gate welcoming the newest graduates into the CLSC. The parade culminates in the Hall of Philosophy for the graduation ceremony.

THE CLSC PARADE

The Chautauqua Literary and Scientific Circle (CLSC), founded in 1878, is the oldest continuous book club in the United States. It has enrolled more than a half-million readers. Each graduating class adopts its own motto and designs a banner emblazoned with class year and motto. Every summer, on Recognition Day, the classes parade along the Red Brick Walk carrying their hand-crafted banners while reciting class mottoes as they proceed toward the Hall of Philosophy.

HALL OF PHILOSOPHY

The Hall of Philosophy is a
popular place to spend part
of an afternoon listening to a
lecture. This open-air facility,
completed in 1906, has a seating
capacity of 700.

The Miller Bell Tower

Built in 1911 to honor co-founder Lewis Miller, this 69-foot Italianate or Tuscan Villa style tower is supported by 100-feet-deep piles. A total of fourteen bells hang in its belfry, totaling over six tons. The largest, the Lewis Miller Bell, weighs 3,033 pounds.

Until recently the pealing of the Miller Bell was performed manually by tugging an attached rope for two minutes prior to Amphitheater programs. Now the five-bell peal is played automatically. During the season the Westminster Chimes can be heard every fifteen minutes from 8:00 AM to 10:00 PM.

The familiar chimes drift throughout the grounds, a gentle reminder to all Chautauquans of the passage of time.

INSIDE THE BELL TOWER

During the season the chime master, Thomas Wierbowski, sits in the base of the tower surrounded by Bell Tower relics, playing tunes on the bells for fifteen minutes, three to four times daily. The curious are welcome to observe and, if lucky, will be regaled with Bell Tower lore.

(OVERLEAF) SUNRISE

Sailboat Races

The Chautauqua Yacht Club sponsors three days of races weekly during the season. Lightenings, Flying Scots, and the largest C Scow fleet in the country compete once the committee boat fires the starting gun.

The weekend races are a great excuse for boaters to spend the day on the lake watching the sailboats jockey for position as they round each mark.

Beaches

There are four public, guarded swimming beaches within the grounds. Heinz Beach, located on the south end, is a popular spot for sunbathing on the docks and swimming laps within the ropes. Children love playing in the oversized sandbox.

CHAUTAUQUA BELLE

The Chautauqua Belle, a steam-powered paddle wheeler, has been a familiar sight on the lake since 1976. Children wave to entice the captain to blow its steam whistle.

SAILING CLASS FOR ADULTS

No matter how old you are, if you want to learn how to sail you can. Here, a class offered by the Sports Club is taught the fundamentals.

ALBERT H. "DOC" SHARPE
PLAYING FIELD

The intra-Chautauqua softball league has games throughout the season. The competitive spirit is fierce, yet friendly.

BICYCLES

Limited access is given to cars inside the gates, so young Chautauquans are free to ride bicycles around the grounds safely.

GOING FISHIN'

HUKILL-LACEY COTTAGE
CIRCA 1880

Sunrise greets these cottages along
the promenade just above South
Lake Drive.

40 SOUTH LAKE DRIVE

YOUTH ACTIVITIES CENTER
(YAC) DANCE ON THE HEINZ
BEACH VERANDA

YAC, located on the top of
the Heinz Beach Bathing
House, is open to junior high
and high school students.

"HANGING OUT" AT THE COLONNADE

55 NORTH LAKE DRIVE

Parties at the President's House are coveted invitations and provide the opportunity to meet and converse with prominent speakers and distinguished guests of the Institution.

BALLET STUDENTS

Ballet students paint their toe shoes as they prepare for an upcoming recital.

PRACTICE SHACK

TIMING AT NORTON HALL

114

PRACTICE . . . PRACTICE . . . PRACTICE

THE ATHENAEUM HOTEL

Built in 1881, it represents the
"American-Victorian Summer
Hotel Style" and was one of the
first commercial buildings in
the world to have electricity.

Traci Gilchrest

Chautauqua Ballet Company

The Chautauqua Ballet Company, under the direction of Dance Artistic Director Jean-Pierre Bonnefoux, presents "An evening of Pas de Deux." The Ballet Company is composed of fifteen professional dancers from companies nationwide and treats the Amphitheater audience to four performances each summer.

DON QUIXOTE

Hernan Justo and Kristi Capps perform a pas de deux from "Don Quixote."

. . . ING

Guest artists Terese Capucilli and Donlin Foreman perform ". . . Ing" with music by Johannes Brahms.

CARMEN

"Carmen" is performed under the stage direction of Johnathon Pape.

The Chautauqua Opera Company presents four operas during the season. All operas are performed in English, following the request of the O. W. Norton family, who donated Norton Memorial Hall in 1929.

BACKSTAGE

Backstage at Norton Memorial Hall where the "Street Urchins" kill time between scenes.

ANTIGONE

The Chautauqua Conservatory Theater Company presents a guest artist production of "Antigone," directed by Derek Anson Jones.

HIGGINS HALL (CHAUTAUQUA CINEMA)
CIRCA 1895

Originally designed as a lecture hall, later utilized as a church, today it is the home of the Chautauqua Cinema. Going to the movies here is a bit nostalgic, seated under the hammer-beam truss ceiling, with the smell of popcorn and days gone by in the air.

14 PECK AVENUE

THE SMITH MEMORIAL
LIBRARY AT NIGHT
CIRCA 1931
This Neo-Georgian
Revival–style building, which
houses 21,000 volumns, stands
on the south side of Bestor
Plaza.

SOUTH TERRACE AVENUE

124

MILLER PARK

These cottages line the north side of Miller Park, the original site of the outdoor auditorium during the early Chautauqua Assemblies. Located down the hill from Bestor Plaza, this park was named for co-founder Lewis Miller.

PACKARD MANOR CIRCA 1917

Inspired by Winston Churchill's country home "Chartwell" in Kent, England, William Doud Packard built this lakeside Tudor mansion. William Packard, of the Packard Motor Company, hired the prestigious architectural firm Warren & Whitmore of New York City, the same firm that designed New York City's Grand Central Terminal.

Packard's fear of fire provided the motivation for his mandate to construct the Manor to be as fireproof as possible. Its walls are solid concrete, and each floor is one-and-a-half feet thick. The exterior brick was imported from England and the slate roof from Belgium.

Packard, who was blind as a result of an insect bite he received while traveling abroad, commissioned a duplicate house to be built in his hometown of Warren, Ohio. It has also been said that he had a speaker-wire that ran from the Amphitheater to his mansion so he could listen to the lectures in the comfort of his Chautauqua home.

The Packard Manor, recently purchased by the Lenna family of Jamestown, New York, has undergone a major restoration and renovation. Each of the 20,909 slate roof tiles were removed and numbered for reinstallation. Some of the larger slate tiles weigh up to 36 pounds.

MAIN GATE TENNIS COURTS

Co-founder John H. Vincent became acquainted with lawn tennis during a visit to England. Upon his return to Chautauqua he commissioned courts to be built. Tennis has been a part of Chautauqua since 1878. Today a daily lottery is held at 5:00 PM sharp to determine the next day's court assignments.

ENGLISH ELLIPTICAL
BOWLS

FOREST IRWIN BOWLING GREEN

Lawn bowling has been a part of
Chautauqua since 1935. The green is
named for a longtime president of the
club. Members carry on the tradition
of wearing whites on Wednesdays.

Boys' and Girls' Club

Located on the lakefront, this is the oldest day camp in the nation. The Boys' Club was founded in 1893 while the Girls' Club commenced in 1895. They combined in 1922. "Club" provides a range of activities for six- to fifteen-year-olds, including field activities, crafts, sailing, kayaking, swimming instruction, and music. A healthy rivalry has existed between the Red and Blue teams for generations.

SPORTS CLUB

The Sports Club has been around since 1942. The club provides facilities for lawn bowling, shuffleboard, bridge, and offers boat rentals so visitors can take advantage of the lake.

HOLY LAND

During the season, tours of Palestine Park are conducted twice a week. Commissioned in 1875 by co-founder John H. Vincent, Palestine Park was designed to teach biblical history and geography. It is built to scale, using small plaster models to represent towns and cities, while Chautauqua Lake is the Mediterranean Sea.

WALKING AROUND THE
GROUNDS

(OVERLEAF) LOOKING OVER
UNIVERSITY BEACH

Autumn in Chautauqua brings

the smells of . . .
burning leaves, first fireplace fires, mulled cider, and

the sounds of . . .
rustling leaves, banter of construction workers, gusting winds, snaps of cottage
tarps, honking geese at dusk, and the chimes of the Miller Bell Tower.

THE MILLER BELL TOWER

137

THE CHAUTAUQUA BOOKSTORE
ON BESTOR PLAZA

MAPLE TREE AT MARKET GATE

Amphitheater

The Amphitheater, under its 1.3-acre roof, hibernates in the off-season.

(OVERLEAF) LOOKING NORTH OF THE BELL TOWER
TOWARD NORTH LAKE DRIVE

PRESIDENT'S HOUSE

The President's House, built in 1985, sits at the bottom of University Hill on North Lake Drive.

6 COOKMAN AVENUE

CIRCA 1879

This clapboard-style cottage is just up the hill from the lake.

JEWETT HOUSE CIRCA 1886

Decorative window on the
highest gable of the Jewett
House on Pratt and
McClintock streets.

DOORWAY TO THE SAMPLE
BOATHOUSE

61 PALESTINE AVENUE

WEDDINGS

The Hall of Philosophy, styled after the Parthenon, is a romantic venue for wedding ceremonies. Towering trees shade the timber roof supported by sixteen Doric columns.

CHAPEL OF THE GOOD SHEPHERD CIRCA 1894

The red door with hand-forged strap hinges beckons everyone who passes this country Gothic chapel. Its wooden pews cozily seat 90.

BAGPIPER PIPING ON HIS WAY
TO A WEDDING CEREMONY

WEDDING ATTENDANTS

HALL OF CHRIST

The Hall of Christ, with its grand classical portico supported by four Ionic columns, provides a gorgeous setting for this bridal party. This structure was designed by Paul J. Pelz, architect of the Library of Congress, and completed in 1909. It was restored and renovated in 1967.

Golf Course

Located across from the Main Gate, the 36-hole Chautauqua Golf Club overlooks the lake. Golf began as early as 1896 at Chautauqua, when a nine-hole "links" course was constructed.

On this autumn day, the thirteenth hole on the Hill Course is surrounded by a medley of fall foliage.

BESTOR PLAZA FOUNTAIN

In the center of Bestor Plaza sits a fountain sculpted by Fred M. Torey. Its four sides depict Art, Music, Religion, and Knowledge.

BOOKSTORE

The Chautauqua Bookstore, on the ground floor of the Post Office Building, is open year round. In addition to selling books, newspapers, magazines, and gifts, it becomes the social center during the off-season.

THE CAREY COTTAGE INN ON BOWMAN AVENUE

WENSLEY GUESTHOUSE CIRCA 1881

This guesthouse, graced by three
stories of wraparound porches, was
donated to Chautauqua by Nina T.
Wensley in 1966. The Wensley provides
lakeside accommodations for some of
the Institution's speakers and enter-
tainers.

ELIZABETH S. LENNA HALL
CIRCA 1993

This 500-seat recital hall for chamber music also provides rehearsal space for the Music School Festival Orchestra and the Chautauqua Symphony Orchestra.

NORTON HALL CIRCA 1929

Home of the Chautauqua Opera Company, this 1,365-seat art deco jewel is filled to capacity during its four productions each season.

Fishing

Fishing is a year-round sport on Chautauqua Lake. Some of its 35 species include bass, perch, bullheads, and the elusive muskellunge, which can weigh up to 40 pounds.

SHERWOOD STUDIO

The Sherwood Studio was built in 1912 as a memorial to the first head of Chautauqua's Piano Department, William H. Sherwood. Classrooms and a small recital hall are housed in this studio.

Tuscan Columns

Of the five classical orders of architecture, the Tuscan column is a simplified form of the typically fluted Doric column.

UNITED CHURCH OF CHRIST
HEADQUARTERS

21 HAWTHORNE AVENUE

THUNDER BRIDGE

Thunder Bridge, named for the sound its wooden slats create as a bicycle rides across it, has given children and those young at heart a thrill for generations.

SEAVER GYM WINDOW

WALKING THE DOG

(OVERLEAF) 8 SOUTH LAKE DRIVE

Wintertime in Chautauqua brings

the smells of . . .
cold crisp air, smoking chimneys, hot cocoa, and

the sounds of . . .
clopping hooves of horses pulling sleighs, ice-skate blades cutting ice, Christmas
carols, gleeful screams of children sledding, swish of cross-country skis, sleigh
bells ringing, crackling fires, crunch and squeek of frozen snow, church bells,
snow pelting on windowpanes, and the chimes of the Miller Bell Tower.

THE MILLER BELL TOWER

46 COOKMAN CIRCA 1905

4 FOREST AVENUE CIRCA 1889

LINCOLN PARK
CONDOMINIUMS

(OVERLEAF) 44 SOUTH LAKE CIRCA 1896

The Adamesque swags combined with fluted,
Ionic-columned porches create an interesting
architectural mix.

CROSS-COUNTRY SKIING
ON BESTOR PLAZA

COOKMAN AVENUE

THUNDER BRIDGE

NORTH LAKE DRIVE

PRATT AVENUE

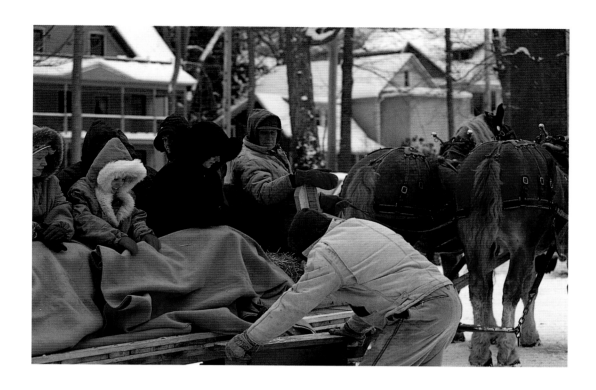

SLEIGH RIDES

43 PRATT AVENUE CIRCA 1994

ARTS & CRAFTS
QUADRANGLE

The shingle-style School of
Art sits on the highest
elevation on the grounds.

BOY WITH RECORDER

A bronze sculpture by H. Richard
Duhme, Jr., located behind the
Smith Memorial Library.

92 NORTH LAKE DRIVE
JAHRLING HOUSE NAMED
BRIGADOON CIRCA 1989

SAMUEL H. HARPER PARK

These cottages border the
Samuel H. Harper Park, fond-
ly called Crosswalk Park, and
are located near the main
gate.

8 HURST CIRCA 1918

This bungalow-style cottage is constructed of fieldstone with brown-stained shingles.

23 HAWTHORNE AVENUE

A Swiss chalet–style cottage built in 1922.

SLEDDING DOWN
UNIVERSITY HILL

PRATT AVENUE

THE MERRY CHRISTMAS HOUSE:
CORNER OF MILLER AND
PALESTINE AVENUES

WINTER WALKS

FOOTBALL ON
SHARPE FIELD

CROSS-COUNTRY SKIING ON
NORTH LAKE DRIVE

NORTH LAKE DRIVE

25 WAUGH AVENUE

27 RAMBLE AVENUE

(OVERLEAF) UNIVERSITY HILL

Bibliography

Bestor, Arthur Eugene, Jr. *Chautauqua Publications: An Historical and Bibliographical Guide.* Chautauqua, N.Y.: Chautauqua Press, 1934.

Bray, Frank Chapin. *A Reading Journey Through Chautauqua.* Chicago: R.R. Donnelly & Sons Company The Lakeside Press, 1905.

Campen, Richard N. *Chautauqua Impressions: Architecture and Ambience.* Chagrin Falls, Ohio: West Summit Press, 1984.

Cram, Mary Frances Bestor. *Chautauqua Salute: A Memoir of the Bestor Years.* Chautauqua, N.Y.: Chautauqua Institution, 1990.

D'Agostino, Anne-Marie. *Chautauqua Porches.* Chautauqua, N.Y.: Sanity Press, 1993.

Edwards, James T. *Pen and Picture: A Chautauqua Sketch-Book.* Meadville, Pa.: The Chautauqua-Century Press, 1896.

Fancher, Pauline. *Chautauqua: Its Architecture and Its People.* Miami, Fla.: Banyan Books, Inc., 1978.

Fox, Joan, and Dorothy Hill. *Walking Tour Guidebook of the Chautauqua Institution.* Chautauqua, N.Y.: Chautauqua Institution, 1999.

Habenicht, Rebecca Sample, and Gracia Habenicht Maley. *Chautauqua Boys' and Girls' Club: Celebrating Our History as the Oldest Daycamp in the Nation 1893-1999.* Chautauqua, N.Y.: Chautauqua Institution, 1999.

Hurlbut, Jesse L. *The Story of Chautauqua.* New York and London: G. P. Putnam's Sons, 1921.

Irwin, Alfreda. *Three Taps of the Gavel: Pledge to the Future.* Chautauqua, N.Y.: Chautauqua Institution, 1987.

Morrison, Theodore. *Chautauqua: A Center of Education, Religion, and the Arts in America.* Chicago and London: University of Chicago Press, 1974.

Richmond, Rebecca. *Chautauqua: An American Place.* New York: Duell, Sloane and Pearce, 1943.

Simpson, Jeffrey. *Chautauqua: An American Utopia.* New York: Harry N. Abrams, Inc. Publishers in association with The Chautauqua Institution, 1999.

Vincent, John Heyl. *The Chautauqua Movement.* Boston: Chautauqua Press, 1885.

The staff of the Chautauqua Institution Archives provided various issues of *The Chautauquan Daily,* Chautauqua pamphlets, and other archival materials that helped me with putting this book together.

Acknowledgments

THANK YOU NEVER SEEMS ENOUGH . . .
A BOOK PROJECT IS A COLLABORATION AND I
WANT TO ACKNOWLEDGE ALL THOSE WHO
HAVE CONTRIBUTED THEIR TIME, EFFORT,
PROFESSIONAL EXPERTISE AND SUPPORT TO
HELP MAKE THIS BOOK A REALITY.

First, I want to thank a person I could not have done this with-out . . . Jon. Although the idea for this book came years ago, Jon was the inspiration I needed to pursue it. From the moment I shared my idea with him he encouraged me . . . from numerous eight-hour commutes to and from Chautauqua, to accompany-ing me on photo shoots, carrying my camera equipment, and editing photos—he was always there for me. Jon also spent *a lot* of time researching and writing the historical introduction . . . not only is he a great husband but he is also a talented writer. Thank you from the bottom of my heart.

Next I'd like to thank Jim Mairs who was the force behind getting my first book, *A Year in Central Park*, published. Once again Jim has offered his time, expertise, contacts, and support and helped to make this book a reality. Thank you for pushing me in directions I may never have ventured.

Jim then introduced me to Katy Homans, who did a beautiful job designing the book and was a joy to work with. Thank you Katy for not only your incredible talent for design but also your guidance.

Jim also introduced me to Nancy Freeman at Mondadori who was instrumental in printing the book. Thank you Nancy.

I also want to thank Joan Fox, director of public information at the Chautauqua Institution, and her assistant Nancy Cummings who have assisted me throughout the project. Thank you for arranging photo permits and putting me in touch with the right people. Joan also did an amazing job factchecking and editing the text, thank you. I truly appreciate your contributions, encouragement, and your continued support.

Richard Redington, vice president for education and planning for the Chautauqua Institution, has been a strong supporter since I presented my idea to him two years ago. Thank you for always promptly answering my emails, your advice, and your encouragement.

I want to also thank Michelle McKenna and Patrick Bernuth who were wonderful in dropping everything to look over layouts, read through copy, and offer advice. Their input was invaluable. A special thank you to Michelle (Mikey . . . Mom) for her amaz-ing talent for editing. We could not have done it without your help.

Another behind-the-scenes editor, Rob Watters. Thank you for your extra hours at the office, back and forth faxes and quick turnaround. Thank you for not only helping with the book but also for the great Chautauqua moments we have shared.

I would also like to give a special thank you to June Miller-Spann, Chautauqua Institution archives manager, and Scott Royer, archives assistant, for all of their time and effort on my behalf . . . I could not have done the research without their assistance.

A number of other people from the Chautauqua Institution have contributed their ideas and encouragement: Daniel Bratton, president, Marty Merkley, vice president for programming, Charles Heinz, vice president for administrative and community services, Gail Whiteman of the Chautauqua Bookstore, and Tom Wierbowski, chime master. Thank you.

I also want to thank my family who are always behind me. My Mom and Dad—Nancy and Charles Watters, Sally, Don, Courtney and Brian Dow, Chuck, Judy, Dirk and Emma Watters, Tim, Margot, Annie, Timmy, Sally and Christopher Watters, and Robert Bruce. Thank you for your unconditional love and support.

Joseph Nassif—I wish I had known about the St. Elmo when you were at the helm. Thank you for your ideas, insights, and enthusiasm during this project.

Lex and Todd Magargee—thank you for your support and encouragement.

HAVING SPENT MY FIRST EIGHT SUMMERS
WORKING AT THE CAREY HOTEL, BOYS' AND
GIRLS' CLUB, THE KOPPER KORNER, AND ON
THE WATERFRONT AS A LIFEGUARD . . . THERE
ARE TOO MANY CHAUTAUQUANS WHO HAVE
CONTRIBUTED TO MY CHAUTAUQUA EXPERI-
ENCE TO MENTION THEM ALL . . . YOU KNOW
WHO YOU ARE . . . THANK YOU.

I do need to mention a few . . . if it weren't for one of my closest friends, Carol Grant McKiernan, I may have never discovered Chautauqua . . . Carol and her family were the first to introduce me to this place that is such a big part of my life. The McKiernan family spend their summers at the lake and have been strong supporters of this book. Thank you.

The Dr. Russell Leslie family—Russ, Ginger, Scott, Lisa, Craig, and Kristen, were a large part of my early summers. I thank you for your continued interest, support, and friendship.

Many other friends—Chautauquans and non-Chautauquans—have offered their encouragement and support and only lack of space precluded me from listing each of you. Thank you.

"Chautauqua . . .

C . H . A . U . T . A . U . Q . U . A .

. . . Chautauqua"